My World of Geography

LAKES

Angela Royston

Heinemann Library
Chicago, Illinois

© 2005 Heinemann Library
a division of Reed Elsevier Inc.
Chicago, Illinois

Customer Service 888-454-2279
Visit our website at www.heinemannlibrary.com

Design: Ron Kamen and Celia Jones
Illustrations: Barry Atkinson (p. 6), Jo Brooker (p. 9),
 Jeff Edwards (pp. 5, 28–29)
Photo Research: Rebecca Sodergren, Melissa Allison, and
 Debra Weatherley
Originated by Ambassador Litho
Printed and bound in China by South
China Printing

09 08 07 06 05
10 9 8 7 6 5 4 3 2 1

**Library of Congress
Cataloging-in-Publication Data**

Royston, Angela.
  Lakes / Angela Royston.
     p. cm. – (My world of geography)
  Includes bibliographical references and index.
  ISBN 1-4034-5591-0 (HC), 1-4034-5600-3 (Pbk)
  1. Lakes–Juvenile literature. I. Title. II. Series.
  GB1603.8.R69 2005
  551.48'2–dc22
                                    2004003866

Acknowledgments

The author and publisher are grateful to the following for permission to reproduce copyright material:
pp. 4, 11, 13, 14, 15, 21 (Dave Houser), 23 (Dale C. Spartas), 26 (Joel W. Rogers) Corbis; pp. 7 (Chris Gallagher), 24 (David Williams) Photo Library Wales; p. 8 John Cleare Mountain Photos; p. 10 Panos Pictures; p. 12 Michael Campbell Photography; pp. 16, 17 Getty Images/Photodisc; pp. 18 (Ian Dagnall), 22 (Pictor/Imagestate) Alamy Images; p. 19 Getty Images/Image Bank; p. 20 NASA; p. 25 Getty Images/Stone; p. 27 (John Noble) Wilderness Photo Library.

Cover photograph reproduced with permission of Corbis/ Ray Juno.

Every effort has been made to contact copyright holders of any material reproduced in this book. Any omissions will be rectified in subsequent printings if notice is given to the publisher.

Contents

Some words are shown in bold, **like this**. You can find out what they mean by looking in the glossary.

What Is a Lake?

A lake is an area of water surrounded by land. Some lakes are small. Others are so big that you cannot see the other side.

This is Lake Arrowhead in California.

This map shows Lake Vänern and Lake Vättern in Sweden.

Lake Vänern

Lake Vättern

SWEDEN

Maps always show lakes as blue shapes in the middle of land. Some lakes may look brown or green in real life, but they are always colored blue on maps.

How Do Lakes Form?

Lakes form when part of the land is lower than other land around it. The lower land makes a bowl shape. Rainwater runs into the bowl and fills it with water.

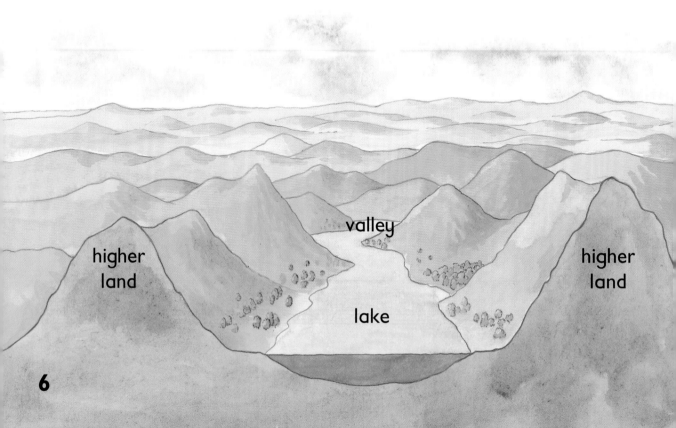

higher land

valley

higher land

lake

Many lakes form in **valleys** between hills and mountains. Water runs down the mountainsides and keeps the lakes full.

Lakes and Rivers

Most lakes are fed by streams and rivers that run into them. Most lakes also have a river or stream flowing out of them. They take away extra water.

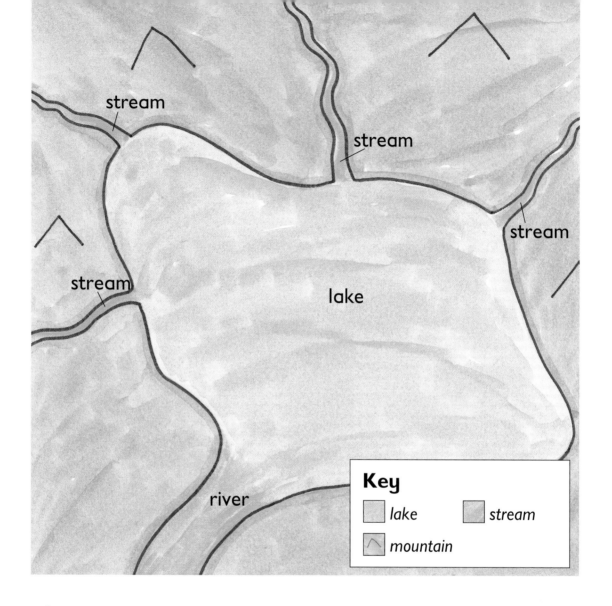

stream

stream

stream

stream

lake

river

Key

lake   stream

mountain

This map shows the streams that run
into the lake on page 8. It also shows
the river that flows out of the lake.
You could draw a map like this.

Using Lake Water

People who live near a lake use the water in many different ways. Farmers may take water from the lake for their **crops.**

This crop is growing near Lake Titicaca in South America.

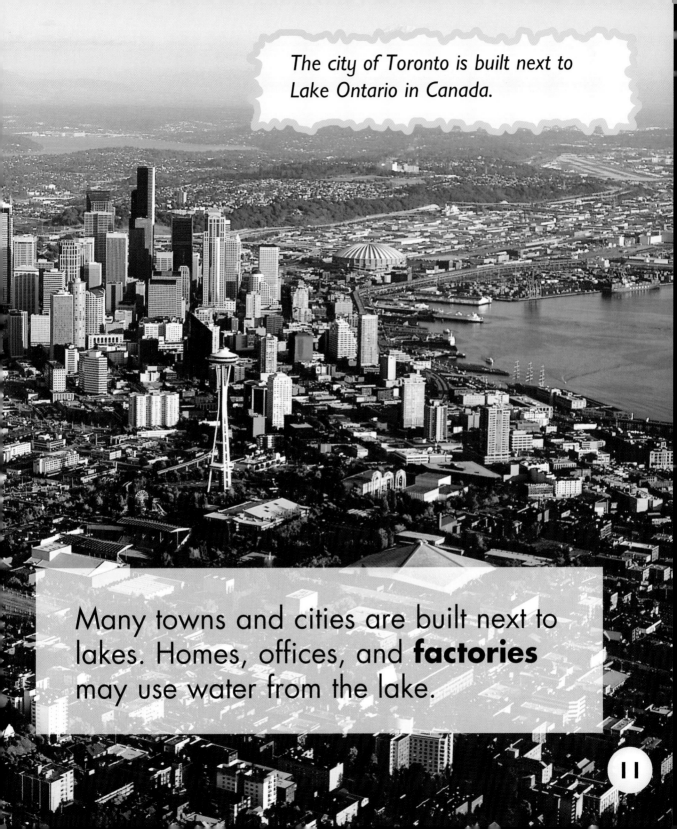

The city of Toronto is built next to Lake Ontario in Canada.

Many towns and cities are built next to lakes. Homes, offices, and **factories** may use water from the lake.

Reservoirs

Sometimes people who live far away from a lake use the water stored in it. This kind of lake is called a **reservoir.** The word *reservoir* means "store of water."

Towns and cities can use water from reservoirs far away. The water flows through pipes laid under the ground. The water is cleaned to make it safe to drink.

Dams

This is Glen Canyon Dam in Arizona.

A **dam** is a thick wall that is built across one end of a river in a **valley.** The valley fills with water to make a **reservoir.**

Special gates are sometimes opened to let some water flow through a dam into a river.

Sometimes a dam is built at one end of a natural lake. The dam stops most of the water from flowing out of the lake.

Making Electricity

Some **dams** are used to make **electricity.** As water from the lake flows through the dam, it turns a huge machine called a **generator.** The generator makes electricity.

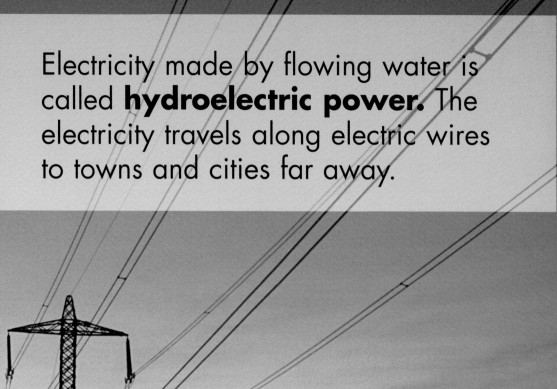

Electricity made by flowing water is called **hydroelectric power.** The electricity travels along electric wires to towns and cities far away.

Traveling on Lakes

Traveling by boat is often the easiest way to get from one part of a lake to another. **Ferries** and **cargo** boats carry people, cars, and **goods.**

Airplanes provide a quick way to travel
to and from lakes that are hard to get to.
Seaplanes have **floats** so that they
can land on and take off from lakes.

Connecting Lakes

The Great Lakes are five huge lakes in North America. Rivers flow from one lake into the next. The St. Lawrence River joins the lakes to the sea.

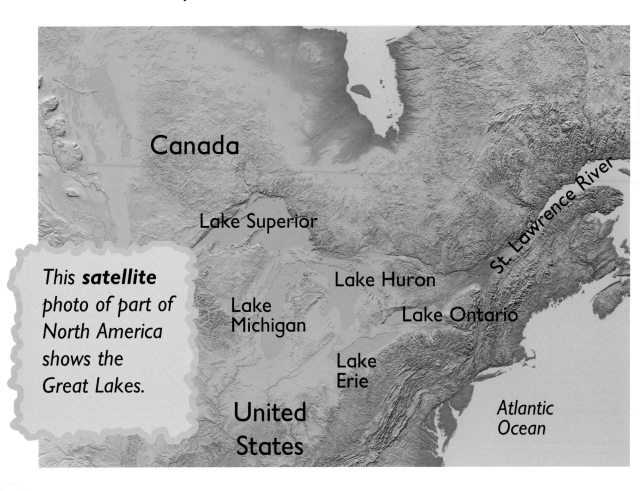

Canada

Lake Superior

St. Lawrence River

Lake Huron

Lake Michigan

Lake Ontario

Lake Erie

Atlantic Ocean

United States

*This **satellite** photo of part of North America shows the Great Lakes.*

In North America, large ships sail from the Atlantic Ocean up the St. Lawrence River. The ships can then sail on to cities on the Great Lakes.

Fishing

Most lakes have fish and other water animals living in them. People who live near lakes catch some of the fish to eat.

These fishers in Southeast Asia are using cages to catch fish.

In some places, people catch the fish that live in the lakes for food. In other places, people catch fish to sell.

Enjoying Lakes

Many people go to lakes for vacations and to enjoy themselves. In summer, some people go to lakes to swim or to fish. Others like to water-ski, windsurf, or use a **canoe**.

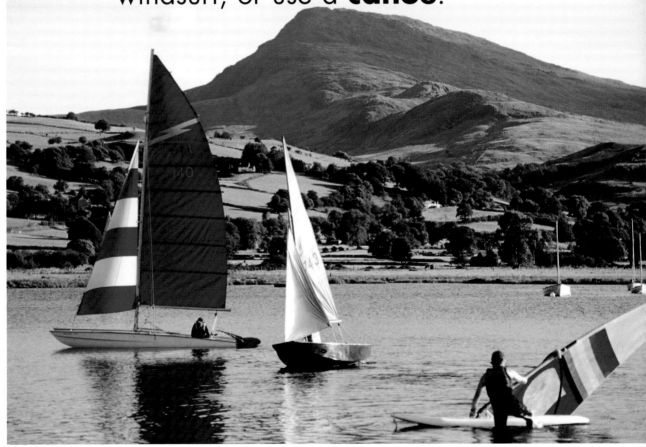

In some very cold places, the **surfaces** of the lakes freeze in winter. Then people can skate on the ice. This lake is in the Netherlands. You should never skate on ice without an adult near by.

Protecting Lakes

Lakes can easily be harmed. **Waste** from **factories** and homes can kill the fish and plants in lakes. People should not get rid of waste by putting it into lakes.

If too much water is taken from a lake or **reservoir,** it begins to dry up. People should try to use less water, especially if the weather is very dry.

Lakes of the World

This map shows the biggest lakes in different parts of the world.

Great Bear Lake
Great Slave Lake

Lake Winnipeg
Lake Superior
Great Lakes

NORTH AMERICA

Lake Superior
Key fact: Lake Superior is the
largest lake in North America.
Size: 31,200 sq miles
         (82,100 sq km)

SOUTH AMERICA

Lake Titicaca

Lough Neagh
Key fact: Lough Neagh is the largest lake in the United Kingdom.
Size: 153 sq miles (396 sq km)

Lake Ladoga
Key fact: Lake Ladoga is the largest lake in Europe.
Size: 6,835 sq miles (17,703 sq km)

Caspian Sea
Key fact: The Caspian Sea is the largest lake in the world.
Size: 143,250 sq miles (371,000 sq km)

Lough Neagh
Loch Ness

EUROPE

Lake Ladoga

Lake Geneva

Lake Baikal

Lake Balkhash

Aral Sea
Caspian Sea

ASIA

AFRICA

Lake Victoria
Lake Tanganyika
Lake Malawi

AUSTRALIA
Lake Eyre

Lake Victoria
Key fact: Lake Victoria is the largest lake in Africa.
Size: 26,828 sq miles (69,484 sq km)

Lake Eyre
Key fact: Lake Eyre is the largest lake in Australia. It contains water only for a short time each year. The rest of the time it is completely dry!
Size: 3,700 sq miles (9,583 sq km)

ANTARCTICA

Glossary

canoe small boat that you move along using a paddle

cargo goods carried by boat or plane

crop plant grown for food

dam thick, high wall at one end of a lake

electricity energy used to make light and heat and to make some engines work

factory place where people make things

ferry boat used to carry people, cars, and other things

float object that floats on water and that helps a larger object float

generator machine that makes electricity

goods things that are made, bought, and sold

hydroelectric power electricity made from flowing water

lock system that allows ships to move between lower and higher parts of a river, canal, or lake

reservoir lake that provides a supply of water for homes, offices, and factories

satellite object put into space that can take photographs or send TV signals, for example

seabed ground at the bottom of the sea

seaplane airplane that can take off and land on water

surface top or outer layer of something

valley low land between two or more hills or mountains

waste leftover materials that people do not want

More Books to Read

Ashwell, Miranda, and Andy Owen. *Lakes.* Chicago: Heinemann Library, 1998.

Ashwell, Miranda, and Andy Owen. *Mountains.* Chicago: Heinemann Library, 1998.

Ashwell, Miranda, and Andy Owen. *Rivers.* Chicago: Heinemann Library, 1998.

Galko, Francine. *Pond Animals.* Chicago: Heinemann Library, 2003.

Sill, Cathryn P., and John Sill. *About Fish: A Guide for Children.* Atlanta: Peachtree Publishers, 2002.

Stille, Darlene R. *Boats.* Minneapolis: Compass Point Books, 2002.

Wade, Mary Dodson. *Types of Maps.* Danbury, Conn.: Scholastic Library, 2003.

Index